Psychedelic Psilocybin Against Cancer Depression

Exploring the Transformative Power in 'Magic Mushrooms' for Patients

Dr. Respira Wise

Table of Content

Introduction

In a world where traditional therapies have often fallen short in addressing the profound depths of human suffering, a remarkable beacon of hope emerges—a transformative path illuminated by the enigmatic allure of psychedelic psilocybin found in **'Magic Mushrooms.'**

Imagine a realm where the insurmountable weight of cancer and the suffocating fog of depression are met with a unique and promising alternative—an avenue where the mysteries of psychedelic therapy intersect with the arduous journeys of patients battling cancer-related depression. Welcome to the realm of ***'Psychedelic Psilocybin Against Cancer Depression - Exploring the Transformative Power in 'Magic Mushrooms' for Patients***,' a journey of healing and discovery that transcends the conventional boundaries of treatment.

This book isn't just a narrative; it's a testament to the profound implications and life-altering potential held within the realms of psychedelic-assisted therapy. It's a testament to the stories of individuals who, in their most vulnerable moments, found solace and profound shifts in their mental and emotional states through the judicious and therapeutic use of psilocybin.

The relevance of this topic is both poignant and pressing. As we navigate the complex labyrinth of cancer, its treatments, and the debilitating specter of depression that often accompanies it, this exploration delves into the uncharted territory of psychedelic therapy. Here, hope resides, intertwined with scientific inquiry, offering an alternative approach that ignites optimism and redefines healing paradigms.

With a perspective rooted in empathy and the amalgamation of scientific exploration and human narratives, this book embarks on a captivating journey. It's a journey that navigates the historical roots of psilocybin use, explores its therapeutic potential, and unravels the intricate mechanisms behind its profound effects on the human psyche.

Through a structured exploration, this book traverses the multifaceted dimensions of psilocybin's impact on cancer patients, delves into the science behind its efficacy, and presents compelling personal accounts that underscore the transformative potential of this therapy. It's a roadmap that not only leads to understanding but also sparks curiosity, inviting readers to explore further and challenge preconceptions about mental health treatment.

For the skeptics and the cautious, rest assured that this exploration is not an invitation to recklessness but a meticulous journey guided by scientific rigor, ethical considerations, and responsible usage. It's a journey that addresses concerns and apprehensions, ensuring clarity and enlightenment rather than fostering fear or uncertainty.

So, dear reader, prepare to embark on a transformative journey—a tantalizing glimpse into the transformative power of 'Magic Mushrooms.' Brace yourself for a riveting exploration that transcends boundaries, challenges norms, and promises a paradigm shift in our understanding of mental health treatment.

Welcome to a world where the seemingly magical touches of 'Magic Mushrooms' hold the potential to offer solace, healing, and hope in the face of adversity.

Buckle up, for the journey is about to begin. This is just the beginning—a mere glimpse into the profound depths waiting to be explored within these pages. The transformative power of psychedelic therapy awaits your discovery.

Chapter 1

Introduction to Psilocybin and Its Healing Potential

Defining Psilocybin and its historical use

Psilocybin is a naturally occurring psychedelic compound found in certain species of mushrooms, often referred to as "magic mushrooms" due to their hallucinogenic properties. Chemically, psilocybin is converted in the body to psilocin, which interacts with serotonin receptors in the brain, leading to altered perception, mood changes, and sometimes profound spiritual experiences.

Historical Roots of Psilocybin Use

The historical use of psilocybin-containing mushrooms traces back through the annals of time, with an intricate arras woven across various cultures worldwide. Particularly prominent in the ancient civilizations of Central and South America, these mushrooms were not merely botanical specimens but held profound significance as conduits to the spiritual realm.

Indigenous Tribes and Ritualistic Practices

Among these cultures, indigenous tribes like the Aztecs, the Mazatecs, and others dwelling in the lush landscapes of Mexico revered these mushrooms as sacred gifts from the Earth. The Aztecs referred to them as "teonanácatl," which translates to "flesh of the gods," signifying their divine connection and esteemed importance.

These indigenous groups integrated psilocybin mushrooms into elaborate religious ceremonies, healing rituals, and spiritual quests. Shamans, revered as spiritual guides and healers within their communities, carefully administered these mushrooms in controlled and sacred settings. The consumption of psilocybin was not merely recreational but served as a means of communion with deities, seeking guidance, healing, and spiritual enlightenment.

Perceived Mysticism and Divine Connection

The experiences induced by ingesting psilocybin-containing mushrooms were perceived as mystical, often characterized by altered states of consciousness, vivid visions, and profound spiritual insights. Participants in these ceremonies reported feeling interconnected with nature, experiencing heightened awareness, and encountering realms beyond the confines of ordinary perception.

The legacy of psilocybin's historical use persists as a testament to the intricate relationship ancient cultures had with these mushrooms. The rediscovery and renewed interest in their therapeutic potential in modern times build upon this rich historical foundation. Understanding the reverence and spiritual significance ancient civilizations attributed to psilocybin offer insights into its potential role in healing and transformation, transcending time and cultural boundaries.

Exploring Psilocybin's Therapeutic Potential

Psilocybin is a naturally occurring psychedelic compound found in certain species of mushrooms. Recent studies have explored the therapeutic potential of psilocybin for various conditions, including depression, anxiety, and addiction, with promising preliminary results

Psilocybin clinical trials

A group of researchers led by Robin L Carhart-Harris explored whether psilocybin, the substance found in magic mushrooms, could help people with a specific type of depression that doesn't respond well to regular treatments. They wanted to check if it was safe and if it actually helped improve the symptoms.

What They Found

Safety: The good news is that all the patients in the study handled psilocybin well. There were no big or unexpected bad reactions or problems, which means it seemed safe for them to take.

Symptom Reduction: The patients' feelings of being down or sad, which are symptoms of depression, got a lot better. Even after a week and three months following the treatment, these improvements were still there. It suggests that the effects of the treatment were lasting.

Improvements in Anxiety and Anhedonia: Not only did the feelings of depression get better, but the patients also reported that their feelings of anxiety and anhedonia (the inability to feel pleasure from things they used to enjoy) improved a lot and these changes lasted over time.

What This Means

The study showed that using psilocybin in patients with this type of tough-to-treat depression was safe, and it seemed to make a real positive difference in how they felt. It's encouraging because it suggests that psilocybin might be a potential treatment option for people with depression that doesn't respond well to other treatments.

Another study found that psilocybin eases psychological distress in people with childhood trauma.

In this study, scientists looked at how psilocybin, the substance found in magic mushrooms, might affect people who experienced difficult or upsetting things during their childhood.

What They Found

Reduced Psychological Distress: The study found that people who had used psilocybin in the last three months felt less upset or troubled compared to those who hadn't used it. This means that psilocybin seemed to help these individuals feel better emotionally.

Effects on Childhood Experiences: Some people go through tough situations during childhood, and these experiences can sometimes cause ongoing distress or emotional pain. The study found that for those who had experienced difficult things during childhood, using psilocybin seemed to have less of a negative effect on their emotions compared to those who didn't use it.

Potential Benefit: The researchers said that this suggests a possible positive effect of psilocybin on helping to ease the emotional burden that comes from difficult childhood experiences. They used the term "potential benefit" because it shows promise that psilocybin could be helpful, but more research is needed to be sure.

What This Means

The study shows that people who had experienced tough times in their childhood and had recently used psilocybin reported feeling less distressed compared to those who didn't use it. This suggests that psilocybin might offer some relief from the emotional difficulties linked to childhood experiences.

Personal accounts and testimonials from clinical trial participants are not widely available in the public domain. However, the studies mentioned above provide preliminary support for the safety and efficacy of psilocybin for various conditions.

Experts discussing mushrooms' effects on the brain.

Psilocybin Study on Brain Activity and Consciousness

The researchers at Imperial College London conducted a study to investigate the impact of psilocybin, the compound present in magic mushrooms, on the brain and consciousness.

Brain Activity during Dream Sleep

Increased Brain Activity: The study discovered that when people were given psilocybin, certain regions of the brain became more active. These specific areas are typically active during dream sleep. It's like psilocybin triggered similar brain patterns that occur when we dream.

Connection to Emotions: These brain areas are part of an ancient system in the brain associated with emotions. So, the increase in brain activity in these regions might indicate that psilocybin affects emotions or feelings in a similar way to how our brains work during dreaming.

Expanded Consciousness

Enhanced Brain Associations: The study also revealed that under the influence of psychedelics like psilocybin, the brain creates a wider range of connections between different thoughts or ideas. This means that the brain becomes more flexible, allowing thoughts to connect more easily.

State of "Expanded" Consciousness: The researchers described this as a state of "expanded" consciousness. This means that under the influence of the drug, the mind becomes more open, making it easier for various thoughts, ideas, or memories to come together and connect.

Implications of the Findings

The study's findings suggest that psilocybin doesn't just affect brain activity but also influences the way our consciousness operates. By enhancing brain activity in regions linked to emotions and allowing for a broader range of connections between thoughts, psilocybin seems to induce a state where the mind can explore different associations more freely.

The research sheds light on how psilocybin alters brain activity, activating regions associated with emotions and fostering an expanded state of consciousness. This provides valuable insight into the mechanisms through which psilocybin might influence emotions and thoughts, offering potential avenues for understanding how it could be used therapeutically.

Chapter 2

Psilocybin's Impact on Cancer Patients

The Healing Potential for Cancer Patients

Psilocybin, the active component in magic mushrooms, has shown promising potential in helping individuals facing the emotional and psychological distress associated with cancer. Beyond its hallucinogenic properties, psilocybin has been increasingly studied for its capacity to offer relief from the emotional burden of cancer diagnoses and treatments.

How Psilocybin Can Help People with Cancer

Alleviating Anxiety and Depression:

Impact of Cancer Diagnosis on Mental Health: A cancer diagnosis can trigger a whirlwind of emotions, leading to intense anxiety, profound sadness, and existential distress. Patients often grapple with the fear of the unknown, the stress of treatment, and the uncertainty surrounding their future.

Psilocybin's Role in Easing Emotional Burden: Studies have indicated that psilocybin, when used in a therapeutic setting, has the potential to mitigate these overwhelming emotions.

It acts on the brain's serotonin receptors, which are associated with regulating mood, and facilitates a unique mental state that allows individuals to confront and work through their emotions.

Sense of Calm and Acceptance: Psilocybin-assisted therapy sessions have shown promising results in offering a profound sense of calm and acceptance. Patients often report feeling more at ease with their diagnosis, experiencing a reduction in anxiety levels, and gaining a greater sense of peace. This shift in perspective can significantly benefit individuals navigating the complexities of cancer treatment.

Enhancing Emotional Coping Mechanisms

Confronting Emotional Toll: Cancer treatment involves not only physical challenges but also emotional and psychological strains. Psilocybin-assisted therapy provides a supportive environment for patients to confront and process these emotional burdens.

Fostering Connection and Perspective Shift: Psilocybin can lead to an expanded state of consciousness, enabling individuals to connect deeply with their emotions and experiences. It allows for a broader perspective on life, helping patients view their situation from a more accepting and less distressing angle.

Acceptance of Life's Uncertainties: Through these therapy sessions, patients often report a newfound acceptance of life's uncertainties. This acceptance is instrumental in helping individuals come to terms with the unpredictability of their illness and the changes it brings to their lives.

Psilocybin's potential in assisting people with cancer lies in its capacity to ease the overwhelming emotions that accompany a diagnosis, offering a sense of calm, acceptance, and peace. Additionally, it aids individuals in processing the emotional toll of the illness by fostering a deeper sense of connection, facilitating perspective shifts, and promoting acceptance of life's uncertainties. These therapeutic benefits may provide invaluable support to individuals navigating the complexities of cancer treatment and improving their overall well-being during this challenging journey.

Studies Highlighting Psychological Benefits for Cancer Patients

Several studies have illuminated the psychological benefits of psilocybin for cancer patients:

Reduction in Anxiety and Depression: Research has shown notable reductions in anxiety and depression levels among cancer patients after undergoing psilocybin-assisted therapy sessions. These individuals reported enhanced mood, reduced fear of death, and improved quality of life.

Increased Sense of Connectedness: Psilocybin has been linked to an increased sense of interconnectedness and spirituality among cancer patients. This feeling of connection often leads to a profound sense of peace and acceptance.

Cautions and Considerations
Some Cautions about Mushrooms and Psilocybin:

Legal Status and Regulatory Concerns: Firstly, it's important to note that psilocybin mushrooms are classified as illegal substances in many countries. Their possession, use, or distribution can result in legal consequences. Understanding the legal landscape in one's area is essential before considering any use.

Potential for Adverse Reactions: Like any psychoactive substance, psilocybin can lead to a range of effects, some of which might be distressing. These may include feelings of anxiety, paranoia, confusion, or even a "bad trip." Individuals with a history of mental health issues, such as psychosis or severe anxiety, may be at higher risk for adverse reactions.

Environmental and Identification Concerns: Gathering wild mushrooms for consumption carries risks due to potential misidentification. Consuming the wrong species of mushrooms can lead to severe poisoning and adverse health effects. Proper identification or seeking mushrooms from reliable sources is crucial for safety.

Addressing Safety Concerns and Potential Risks Associated with Usage:

Setting and Supervision: Psilocybin use should take place in a safe and controlled environment, ideally under the guidance of trained professionals in a therapeutic or ceremonial setting. The setting greatly influences the overall experience, and having a trusted guide can help manage potential challenges.

Dosage and Individual Sensitivity: Determining the appropriate dosage is critical, as individual responses to psilocybin can vary significantly. Factors such as body weight, metabolism, and personal tolerance influence how someone reacts to the substance. Starting with a low dose and gradually increasing, known as "start low, go slow," is advisable to gauge individual sensitivity.

Medical Considerations and Drug Interactions: Individuals with underlying medical conditions, especially heart conditions or those taking medications, should exercise caution. Psilocybin may interact with certain medications, leading to adverse effects. Consulting a healthcare professional before use is essential to assess potential risks and interactions.

Potential Long-term Effects: The long-term effects of regular or high-dose psilocybin use are not yet fully understood. Continued use may lead to tolerance, dependence, or psychological effects that persist beyond the acute experience.

While psilocybin has shown therapeutic promise, it's crucial to approach its use with caution. Awareness of legal implications, potential adverse reactions, environmental considerations, setting, dosage, individual sensitivity, medical considerations, and long-term effects are essential for ensuring safety and minimizing risks associated with psilocybin use. Seeking guidance from trained professionals, maintaining a respectful approach, and being well-informed are key factors in maximizing potential benefits while minimizing potential harms.

Chapter 3

Depression and Lifestyle Factors

Understanding Depression and Lifestyle Habits

Depression is a mood disorder characterized by profound feelings of sadness, isolation, hopelessness, or emptiness. It affects everyone differently, but it can interfere with your daily activities, work, and life in general.

Understanding depression involves exploring its multifaceted nature, encompassing biological, psychological, and social factors that contribute to its onset and progression. Additionally, recognizing the influence of lifestyle habits on mental health plays a crucial role in managing and preventing depression.

The Complex Nature of Depression:

Depression is more than occasional feelings of sadness or low mood. It's a complex mental health condition characterized by persistent feelings of sadness, hopelessness, and a lack of interest in activities that once brought joy. Understanding depression involves acknowledging its diverse causes, which can vary from person to person.

Biological Factors:

Biological factors contribute significantly to depression. Neurotransmitter imbalances, particularly involving serotonin, norepinephrine, and dopamine, play a role in regulating mood. Additionally, genetics and family history of mental health disorders can predispose individuals to depression.

Psychological Factors:

Psychological elements also contribute to depression. Trauma, chronic stress, low self-esteem, and negative thought patterns can exacerbate symptoms or trigger depressive episodes. Understanding one's emotional triggers and patterns is crucial in managing depression effectively.

Social Factors:

Social factors, such as isolation, lack of social support, financial stressors, and relationship difficulties, can significantly impact mental health. Social connections and a supportive network are vital in preventing and managing depression.

Healthy lifestyle habits to prevent depression, new study finds

Several lifestyle habits can help prevent the onset or worsening of mental health conditions, including depression. A recent study published in the journal Nature Mental Health identified seven healthy lifestyle factors that reduce the risk of depression. These factors include:

Having a Healthy Diet:

Eating a balanced diet that includes fatty acids, omega-3s, omega-6s, branched-chain amino acids, and micronutrients such as magnesium, folic acid, B6, and B12 can help prevent depression.

Nutrient-Rich Foods and Depression Prevention:

Fatty Acids (Omega-3s and Omega-6s): Consuming foods rich in omega-3 fatty acids (such as fish, flaxseeds, and walnuts) and omega-6 fatty acids (found in vegetable oils and seeds) is linked to reduced rates of depression. These fatty acids play a role in brain function and mood regulation.

Branched-Chain Amino Acids: Foods containing branched-chain amino acids (BCAAs), like lean meats, dairy products, and legumes, contribute to the synthesis of neurotransmitters involved in mood regulation.

Micronutrients (Magnesium, Folic Acid, B6, B12): Adequate intake of micronutrients, including magnesium, folic acid, and B vitamins (B6 and B12), is associated with a lower risk of depression. These nutrients are involved in neurotransmitter synthesis and brain function.

Balanced Diet and Mental Health:

A balanced diet consisting of a variety of fruits, vegetables, whole grains, lean proteins, and healthy fats provides essential nutrients that support brain health. Such a diet can positively impact mood, cognitive function, and overall mental well-being, reducing the risk of depression.

Regular Physical Activity:

Exercise increases your body's production of natural antidepressants. Exercising for 30 minutes a day, three to five days a week, may increase your resilience against stressful stimuli without the use of medication. It can help reduce stress, improve mood, boost self-esteem, and provide restful sleep.

Antidepressant Effects of Exercise:

Natural Antidepressants: Physical activity stimulates the release of endorphins and neurotransmitters like dopamine and serotonin, known as natural antidepressants. These chemicals contribute to improved mood and reduced feelings of stress and anxiety.

Stress Reduction and Mood Enhancement: Engaging in regular exercise, even for moderate durations (30 minutes a day, three to five days a week), has been shown to reduce stress levels, improve mood, boost self-esteem, and enhance overall mental resilience.

Quality Sleep and Self-Esteem: Exercise helps in achieving restful sleep, which is crucial for mental health. Furthermore, the sense of accomplishment from regular physical activity can boost self-esteem and confidence.

Avoiding Smoking:

Smoking and Depression Risk:

Studies have found a significant association between smoking and an increased risk of depression. Nicotine in cigarettes affects neurotransmitter levels in the brain, contributing to mood disturbances and an increased vulnerability to depressive symptoms.

Limiting Alcohol Consumption:

Moderate Alcohol Intake and Depression Risk:

Association with Reduced Risk: Moderate alcohol consumption has been associated with a reduced risk of depression. However, this association is nuanced. Consuming alcohol in moderate amounts, such as one drink per day for women and up to two drinks per day for men, may have protective effects against depression.

Potential Mechanisms: Some studies suggest that certain components in alcoholic beverages, like polyphenols in red wine, might have antioxidant and anti-inflammatory properties that could positively influence mood regulation. However, excessive alcohol intake can have adverse effects on mental health and exacerbate depressive symptoms.

Having Frequent Social Connections:

Impact of Social Isolation on Depression:

Reduced Social Connections and Increased Risk: Social isolation or a lack of meaningful social connections is strongly associated with an increased risk of depression. Humans are social beings, and regular social interaction contributes to emotional well-being, reducing feelings of loneliness and isolation.

Benefits of Social Support: Maintaining close relationships, engaging in social activities, and having a support network can provide emotional support, a sense of belonging, and validation, thereby lowering the risk of depression.

Getting Adequate Sleep:

Sleep Quality and Depression Risk:

Association with Increased Risk: Sleep deprivation or poor sleep quality is closely linked to an increased risk of depression. Insufficient sleep disrupts mood-regulating neurotransmitters and hormone levels, leading to emotional instability and an increased vulnerability to depressive symptoms.

Importance of Sleep Hygiene: Prioritizing good sleep hygiene, which includes establishing a regular sleep schedule, creating a comfortable sleep environment, and practicing relaxation techniques before bedtime, plays a crucial role in maintaining mental well-being and preventing depression.

Keeping Sedentary Behavior to a Minimum:

Impact of Sedentary Lifestyle on Mental Health:

Association with Increased Risk: Sedentary behavior, characterized by prolonged sitting and minimal physical activity, is associated with a higher risk of depression. Lack of movement and exercise can lead to reduced production of mood-regulating neurotransmitters and increased feelings of stress and anxiety.

Promoting Physical Activity: Engaging in regular physical activity, even in moderate amounts, can counteract sedentary behavior and its associated negative effects on mental health. Exercise releases endorphins, reduces stress, and contributes to an overall positive mood.

In addition to these lifestyle habits, other factors such as **exposure to abuse**, **emotional attachment**, **work environment**, and **meditation and relaxation techniques** can also affect a person's mental health. It is important to note that while these lifestyle habits can help prevent depression, they should not be considered a substitute for professional medical advice. If you are experiencing symptoms of depression, please consult with a licensed healthcare professional.

Risk factors for depression

Common risk factors and their significance

Family History and Genetics

Inherited Risk Factors:

Increased Risk with Family History: Having a close family member, like a parent or sibling, diagnosed with depression significantly raises an individual's risk. Genetics play a role in predisposing individuals to depression, and having a family history can increase this risk by 2 to 3 times compared to those without a family history.

Genetic Susceptibility: Certain genetic variations or alterations can influence neurotransmitter function, brain structure, or the body's stress response system. These genetic predispositions, when combined with environmental factors, can contribute to the development of depression.

Chronic Stress

Impact on Stress Response and Mental Health:

Normal vs. Chronic Stress: Stress, in small doses, can serve as a motivator and help individuals cope with challenges. However, chronic stress overwhelms the body's stress response system, leading to wear and tear on physical and mental health.

Stress and Brain Chemistry: Prolonged exposure to stress hormones, like cortisol, can disrupt neurotransmitter levels in the brain, affecting mood regulation. Chronic stress weakens the body's ability to cope, making individuals more vulnerable to developing depression.

History of Trauma

Link Between Trauma and Depression:

Increased Vulnerability: Individuals who have experienced trauma, such as physical or sexual abuse, neglect, or violence, are at a heightened risk of developing depression. Traumatic experiences can lead to persistent emotional distress and impact one's mental health.

Effect on Brain Function: Trauma can alter brain structure and function, particularly in areas involved in emotion regulation and stress response. This alteration may lead to an increased susceptibility to mood disorders like depression.

Gender

Gender Disparities in Depression:

Higher Prevalence in Women: Women are approximately twice as likely as men to experience depression. This difference may be attributed to various factors including biological, hormonal, psychological, and sociocultural influences.

Hormonal and Biological Factors: Hormonal fluctuations during menstruation, pregnancy, postpartum, and menopause can affect neurotransmitter levels, potentially increasing vulnerability to depression in women. Additionally, social and cultural expectations, such as caregiving roles, may contribute to increased stress and risk of depression.

Poor Nutrition

Dietary Deficiencies and Depression Risk:

Impact of Essential Nutrients: A diet lacking essential nutrients, particularly omega-3 fatty acids found in fish, flaxseeds, and walnuts, has been linked to an increased risk of depression. Omega-3s play a role in brain health and mood regulation.

Micronutrients and Mood: Inadequate intake of micronutrients like B vitamins (such as B6 and B12), magnesium, and folate can impact neurotransmitter production, potentially affecting mood and increasing the risk of depression.

Unresolved Grief or Loss

Grieving Process and Depression:

Triggering Emotional Distress: Significant losses, like the death of a loved one, divorce, or other major life changes, can trigger profound emotional distress. Unresolved grief or ongoing feelings of loss can lead to prolonged periods of sadness, hopelessness, and eventually contribute to depression in some individuals.

Disruption of Emotional Stability: The grieving process can disrupt one's emotional stability, leading to a range of emotional responses that may include depression. The inability to cope with these emotions or to find resolution may intensify the risk.

Personality Traits

Impact of Specific Traits on Depression:

Low Self-Esteem and Pessimism: Individuals with low self-esteem or a pessimistic outlook may be more susceptible to depressive symptoms. Negative self-perceptions and a consistently negative view of the world can contribute to feelings of hopelessness and helplessness.

Being Overly Self-Critical: Those who are overly self-critical or self-blaming may experience higher levels of stress and ruminate on negative thoughts, increasing vulnerability to depression.

It is important to note that while these risk factors can increase the likelihood of developing depression, they do not necessarily cause depression. Depression is a complex disorder with multiple factors weighing in. If you are experiencing symptoms of depression, please consult with a licensed healthcare professional.

Chapter 4

Mechanisms of Psilocybin's Action

How Psilocybin Works in the Brain

Psilocybin is a non-selective agonist at many serotonin receptors, especially at serotonin 5-HT 2A receptors, and is found in the Psilocybe genus of mushrooms. The pharmacodynamic mechanisms mediating the antidepressant and psychedelic effects of psilocybin are currently unknown but are thought to involve the modulation of the serotonergic system, primarily through agonism at the 5-HT 2A receptors and downstream changes in gene expression. It is also established that indirect effects on dopaminergic and glutamatergic systems are contributory, as well as effects at other lower affinity targets.

Let's break down and elaborate on how psilocybin functions within the brain:

Serotonin Receptor Agonism: Psilocybin, present in certain mushroom species like Psilocybe, acts as a non-selective agonist, binding to various serotonin receptors in the brain. Notably, it has a high affinity for the serotonin 5-HT2A receptors, triggering specific signaling pathways.

5-HT2A Receptor Modulation: Psilocybin's primary action involves stimulating serotonin 5-HT2A receptors. This activation initiates a cascade of neural events, altering the flow of information across neural networks, especially in areas associated with mood regulation, perception, and cognition.

Serotonergic System Modulation: The exact mechanisms behind psilocybin's antidepressant and psychedelic effects remain unclear. However, it is believed that its actions involve modulation of the serotonergic system. Psilocybin's interaction with 5-HT2A receptors is thought to induce downstream changes in gene expression, leading to alterations in neuronal function and connectivity.

Indirect Effects on Neurotransmitter Systems: Psilocybin's impact extends beyond serotonin modulation. It indirectly affects other neurotransmitter systems, including dopamine and glutamate. These secondary effects contribute to its complex neural modulation and may play a role in its therapeutic actions.

Other Targets: Psilocybin exhibits effects on various brain targets beyond serotonin receptors. While less selective, these interactions at lower affinity targets may contribute to its overall impact on brain function, influencing mood, cognition, and perception.

Impact and Therapeutic Potential

Antidepressant Effects: By modulating the serotonergic system, particularly through agonism at 5-HT2A receptors, psilocybin shows promise in alleviating symptoms of depression. The alterations in neural pathways and gene expression induced by psilocybin may contribute to its potential antidepressant effects.

Psychedelic Effects: The activation of 5-HT2A receptors by psilocybin triggers changes in perception, cognition, and consciousness, leading to the psychedelic experience. This altered state of consciousness, characterized by visual and sensory alterations, may facilitate introspection and emotional processing, potentially aiding in therapeutic interventions.

Detailed breakdown of psilocybin's effects on neural pathways.

Psilocybin alters neural circuitry and key brain regions previously implicated in depression, including the default mode network and amygdala.

Altering Default Mode Network (DMN):

Psilocybin influences the default mode network (DMN), a collection of brain regions active during rest and self-referential thoughts. In depression, the DMN may exhibit hyperactivity and abnormalities. Psilocybin decreases the activity in the DMN, disrupting its normal functioning. This alteration may lead to changes in self-referential thoughts and a shift in consciousness, potentially contributing to its therapeutic effects.

Modulating the Amygdala:

The amygdala, vital in emotion processing and regulation, is implicated in mood disorders like depression. Psilocybin increases activity in the amygdala, potentially influencing emotional processing. This increased activity might facilitate the processing of emotions, including fear and anxiety, which could contribute to the antidepressant effects by aiding emotional regulation and processing.

Impact on Brain-Derived Neurotrophic Factor (BDNF) and Neurogenesis:

Enhancing BDNF Production:

Psilocybin's interaction with serotonin receptors, notably 5-HT2A agonism, leads to increased production of brain-derived neurotrophic factor (BDNF) in the hippocampus. BDNF plays a crucial role in neuronal growth, survival, and synaptic plasticity, which are essential for mood regulation and cognitive function. The increase in BDNF production might contribute to the therapeutic effects of psilocybin by supporting neuronal health and adaptive neural changes.

Neurogenesis and Fear Extinction:

Psilocybin-induced neurogenesis in the hippocampus, coupled with the increase in BDNF, may facilitate the extinction of conditioned fear-related behaviors. This phenomenon can aid in reducing fear responses and promote adaptive learning, potentially benefiting individuals with depression and anxiety disorders.

Serotonergic and Glutamatergic Systems in Prefrontal Circuits:

Interplay Between Serotonin and Glutamate:

Psilocybin's therapeutic effects in depressive and anxiety states are believed to involve a complex interplay between the serotonergic and glutamatergic systems in prefrontal circuits. The modulation of these systems might result in alterations in neural circuits that underlie mood regulation and emotional processing.

Prefrontal Circuits and Therapeutic Potential:

Psilocybin's impact on prefrontal circuits, encompassing serotonergic and glutamatergic interactions, may contribute to its potential therapeutic effects in depressive and anxiety states. The alterations in these circuits could lead to adaptive changes in mood regulation and emotional responses, potentially ameliorating symptoms of depression and anxiety.

Scientific explanations of psilocybin's impact on mood regulation.

Psilocybin's impact on mood regulation is thought to involve the modulation of the serotonergic system, primarily through agonism at the 5-HT 2A receptors and downstream changes in gene expression.

Modulation of the Serotonergic System:

Agonism at 5-HT 2A Receptors:

Psilocybin primarily acts by binding to and activating serotonin 5-HT 2A receptors in the brain. This interaction triggers a cascade of neural events, altering serotonin signaling pathways. Serotonin, a neurotransmitter associated with mood regulation, plays a pivotal role in emotional processing and mental well-being.

Downstream Gene Expression Changes:

Upon activation of 5-HT 2A receptors, psilocybin induces downstream changes in gene expression. These alterations may lead to modifications in neural connectivity, synaptic plasticity, and neurotransmitter release, potentially influencing mood-related brain circuits.

Impact on Neural Circuitry and Brain Regions:

Alteration of Default Mode Network (DMN):

Psilocybin disrupts the activity of the default mode network (DMN), a collection of brain regions involved in self-referential thoughts and mind wandering. Dysfunctions in the DMN are associated with depression. Psilocybin's ability to decrease DMN activity may lead to changes in self-perception and consciousness, potentially contributing to its mood-altering effects.

Modulation of the Amygdala:

Psilocybin increases activity in the amygdala, a brain region crucial in emotional processing, particularly fear and anxiety. This enhanced activity might facilitate emotional regulation and processing, which could influence mood regulation and potentially alleviate symptoms of depression.

Influence on Brain-Derived Neurotrophic Factor (BDNF) in the Hippocampus:

5-HT 2A Agonist Properties and BDNF Production:

Psilocybin's interaction with 5-HT 2A receptors leads to increased production of brain-derived neurotrophic factor (BDNF) in the hippocampus. BDNF plays a vital role in neuronal growth, synaptic plasticity, and resilience against stress. Elevated BDNF levels might promote adaptive changes in neural circuits involved in mood regulation.

Therapeutic Potential and Further Research:

Complex Mechanisms and Therapeutic Implications:

Psilocybin's multifaceted impact on the serotonergic system, neural circuitry, and brain regions associated with mood regulation hints at its therapeutic potential in modulating mood and potentially treating depression. The interplay of these mechanisms may contribute to its antidepressant effects.

Need for Continued Research:

Despite advancements, further research is essential to comprehensively understand the precise mechanisms of psilocybin's action on mood regulation and depression. A deeper understanding will aid in refining therapeutic interventions and elucidating its potential applications in mental health treatment.

Psilocybin's impact on mood regulation involves its interaction with the serotonergic system, alterations in neural circuitry (such as the DMN and amygdala), and the modulation of BDNF production in the hippocampus. These complex mechanisms collectively contribute to its potential therapeutic effects in mood disorders like depression. Continued research is crucial to unravel the intricacies of psilocybin's actions and its precise role in modulating mood, aiding in the development of novel treatments for mental health conditions.

Chapter 5

Psychedelics in Trauma Therapy

Psychedelics have shown promise in treating various mental health conditions, including depression, anxiety, and addiction. Recent studies have also explored the therapeutic potential of psychedelics for trauma-related disorders such as post-traumatic stress disorder (PTSD).

Addressing Trauma with Psychedelics

Psychedelics such as psilocybin and MDMA have been shown to have therapeutic potential for treating PTSD. Psilocybin is a non-selective agonist at many serotonin receptors, especially at serotonin 5-HT 2A receptors, and is found in the Psilocybe genus of mushrooms.

Therapeutic Potential of Psilocybin:

Mechanism of Action:

Psilocybin, a non-selective agonist primarily activating serotonin 5-HT2A receptors, is found in certain mushrooms like Psilocybe genus. Its mechanisms mediating therapeutic effects, including antidepressant and psychedelic impacts, are not fully elucidated. However, it's believed to modulate the serotonergic system, inducing downstream changes in gene expression.

Agonism at 5-HT2A receptors and potential interactions with dopamine and glutamate systems contribute to its effects. These interactions might facilitate alterations in neural circuits associated with mood regulation, emotion processing, and perception.

Therapeutic Effects on Trauma:

Psilocybin's ability to modulate brain networks implicated in emotional processing, including the amygdala and default mode network (DMN), may help individuals process traumatic memories. The alteration in these neural pathways might facilitate a change in perception and emotional response to traumatic events, potentially alleviating PTSD symptoms.

Therapeutic Potential of MDMA:

Pharmacodynamics:

MDMA, a synthetic compound, increases the release of neurotransmitters like serotonin, dopamine, and norepinephrine in the brain. Its primary mechanism involves enhancing the release of these neurotransmitters, particularly serotonin, which plays a crucial role in mood regulation and emotional processing.

Effects on PTSD:

MDMA has exhibited promising effects in reducing fear and defensiveness while enhancing trust and empathy. These effects may facilitate a therapeutic environment conducive to addressing traumatic experiences in psychotherapy settings.

By reducing fear responses, MDMA-assisted therapy might allow individuals to approach and process traumatic memories with reduced anxiety, potentially enabling deeper therapeutic exploration and resolution of past traumas.

Case studies and expert discussions on treating trauma with psilocybin

Several studies have shown that psilocybin-assisted therapy can be effective in treating PTSD. An open-label study in traumatized AIDS survivors found that psilocybin-assisted psychotherapy reduced PTSD symptoms, attachment anxiety, and demoralization. Several other studies have also shown preliminary efficacy in facilitating confronting traumatic memories, decreasing emotional avoidance, depression, anxiety, pessimism, and disconnection from others, and increasing acceptance, self-compassion, and forgiveness of abusers, all of which are relevant to PTSD recovery.

Effectiveness of Psilocybin-Assisted Therapy:

- *AIDS Survivors Study:* An open-label study conducted with traumatized AIDS survivors demonstrated promising outcomes. Psilocybin-assisted psychotherapy was associated with reduced PTSD symptoms, including attachment anxiety and demoralization. This study highlighted the potential of psilocybin in addressing symptoms relevant to PTSD recovery.

- *Preliminary Efficacy*: Other studies have also shown preliminary efficacy in various aspects related to trauma recovery. These include facilitating the confrontation of traumatic memories, reducing emotional avoidance, depression, anxiety, pessimism, and feelings of disconnection from others.
- *Positive Psychological Changes*: Psilocybin therapy has been associated with increases in acceptance, self-compassion, and forgiveness of abusers. These psychological changes are considered relevant to the recovery process in individuals dealing with trauma-related conditions like PTSD.

Expert Discussions and Insights:

- *Support for Safety and Efficacy*: Expert discussions and case studies provide initial support for the safety and efficacy of psilocybin-assisted therapy in treating PTSD. The observed positive psychological changes suggest a potential for significant therapeutic benefits in trauma recovery.
- *Call for Further Research*: Despite these promising findings, experts emphasize the need for more extensive research to comprehend the mechanisms of action and the long-term effects of psilocybin therapy for trauma treatment. Additional studies are required to establish safety profiles, optimize treatment protocols, and understand potential risks associated with its use.

Important Considerations:

Regulatory Status and Professional Guidance:

Psilocybin and MDMA are classified as controlled substances in many countries due to their psychoactive properties. Their use should only be considered under the guidance of licensed healthcare professionals in controlled settings.

Need for Continued Research:

Further research is crucial to expand our understanding of how psilocybin-assisted therapy works in treating trauma-related conditions. Investigating mechanisms of action, potential risks, optimal dosages, and long-term effects is imperative for establishing evidence-based therapeutic protocols.

Chapter 6

Future Directions in Psychedelic Research

Advancements and Opportunities

Psychedelic therapy is a rapidly evolving field of research with promising potential for treating various mental health conditions. Here are some of the advancements and opportunities in the field:

New treatments for psychiatric and behavioral disorders:

Johns Hopkins Center for Psychedelic and Consciousness Research: Researchers at the Johns Hopkins Center have received substantial funding amounting to $55 million. This funding represents a significant milestone, showcasing growing interest and investment in psychedelic research.

Development of Tailored Treatments:

Targeting Diverse Psychiatric Disorders: The research efforts aim to broaden the scope of psychedelic therapy beyond specific conditions like depression or PTSD. Scientists are exploring the potential of psychedelics to treat a wider range of psychiatric and behavioral disorders.

Personalized Treatment Approaches: Researchers aspire to develop treatments customized to the individual needs of patients. This personalized approach involves tailoring therapies to address unique symptom profiles, responsiveness to treatments, and specific mental health conditions experienced by each patient.

Significance and Potential Impact:

Expanding Treatment Options:

Addressing Unmet Needs: The exploration of psychedelics for psychiatric and behavioral disorders offers a ray of hope for individuals facing treatment-resistant conditions or those with limited effective treatment options. This research endeavors to provide novel therapeutic interventions for conditions that are challenging to treat conventionally.

Advancing Mental Health Care:

Potential Paradigm Shift: If successful, the development of new treatments based on psychedelic therapy could signify a paradigm shift in mental health care. It may introduce alternative, innovative therapeutic approaches that complement or enhance existing treatment modalities.

Future Directions and Considerations:

Clinical Research and Regulatory Challenges:

Robust Clinical Trials: Ongoing and future clinical trials are crucial to validate the safety, efficacy, and long-term effects of psychedelic therapies across diverse mental health conditions. Rigorous research methodologies and large-scale trials are needed to establish credibility and inform treatment guidelines.

Navigating Regulatory Frameworks: The field faces regulatory hurdles due to the historical stigmatization and legal restrictions on psychedelics. Collaborative efforts between researchers, policymakers, and regulatory bodies are essential to navigate these challenges and facilitate the responsible exploration of psychedelic therapies.

Ethical and Safety Considerations:

Ensuring Ethical Practices: Ethical considerations, including informed consent, patient safety, and minimizing risks, are paramount in conducting research and administering psychedelic therapies. Ethical guidelines must be rigorously followed to safeguard patient well-being.

Expanded research in healthy volunteers

Expanding research involving healthy volunteers within the framework of the Johns Hopkins Center for Psychedelic and Consciousness Research marks a significant stride in understanding the potential benefits and impacts of psychedelics beyond clinical applications

Importance of Research in Healthy Volunteers

Understanding Psychedelic Effects:

Exploration Beyond Pathology: Conducting research with healthy volunteers allows scientists to study the effects of psychedelics in individuals without psychiatric conditions. This approach broadens the understanding of how these substances influence cognition, perception, emotions, and consciousness in a non-clinical context.

Exploring Potential Benefits: By focusing on healthy individuals, researchers aim to uncover potential positive effects that psychedelics might have on cognition, creativity, emotional well-being, spirituality, and overall human experience. This exploration goes beyond treating disorders, aiming to unravel ways these substances may enhance human thriving.

Research Objectives and Aspirations

Opening New Avenues:

Promoting Human Thriving: The ultimate goal of this expanded research is to explore how psychedelics might contribute to human thriving and well-being beyond merely treating mental health conditions. It seeks to uncover ways in which these substances might support positive psychological states, personal growth, and overall human flourishing.

Potential Applications: Insights gained from studying healthy volunteers might uncover applications in enhancing creativity, fostering spirituality, improving emotional resilience, facilitating personal development, and nurturing aspects of human experience that contribute to well-rounded thriving and fulfillment.

Ethical Considerations and Methodologies

Ethical Guidelines:

Ensuring Safety and Well-being: Ethical protocols are crucial to safeguard the safety, well-being, and autonomy of healthy volunteers participating in these studies. Strict adherence to ethical guidelines and informed consent procedures is fundamental to protect participants.

Minimizing Risks: Research involving healthy volunteers must be conducted with extreme care to minimize any potential risks associated with psychedelic substances. Researchers must ensure a safe environment, proper screening, and comprehensive monitoring throughout the study process.

Future Implications and Challenges:

Expanding Understanding:

Holistic View of Psychedelics: This expanded research initiative could offer a more comprehensive understanding of the holistic effects of psychedelics, shedding light on their impact on various aspects of human experience and psychology, potentially uncovering new therapeutic avenues.

Navigating Regulatory Frameworks:

Regulatory and Societal Challenges: Despite the potential benefits, conducting research on psychedelics in healthy volunteers may face regulatory and societal challenges due to historical stigmatization and legal restrictions. Navigating these challenges while adhering to ethical guidelines is crucial for the acceptance and progress of this research.

Real-world data collection

Collecting real-world data on psychedelic drug use represents a significant shift in research methodologies, aiming to comprehend the broader context and diverse experiences of individuals using these substances.

Importance of Real-World Data Collection:

Understanding Diverse Experiences:

Broader Contextual Insights: Real-world data collection allows researchers to gather information from a diverse range of individuals using psychedelics outside of controlled clinical settings. This approach helps in understanding how various settings, contexts, and individual psychological states might impact the outcomes of psychedelic experiences.

Incorporating Varied Perspectives: By incorporating real-life experiences, researchers gain insights into the varied ways people use psychedelics, their subjective experiences, and the factors that influence the outcomes. This approach captures a wide spectrum of experiences beyond the controlled environment of clinical trials.

Focus of Data-Driven Approaches

Setting and Psychological State:

Impact of Setting: Researchers aim to understand how the setting, encompassing the physical environment, social context, and emotional atmosphere, influences the psychedelic experience. Factors like safety, comfort, and social support might significantly impact the quality and outcome of the experience.

Psychological State: Assessing the psychological state of individuals before, during, and after psychedelic use is crucial. Variables such as mood, mindset, emotional well-being, and mental preparedness might influence the subjective effects and overall experience.

Insights and Information Dissemination

Informing Psychedelic Users:

Educational and Harm Reduction Efforts: Through data-driven approaches, researchers aspire to inform individuals considering or intending to use psychedelics. Insights derived from real-world experiences can be disseminated to help users understand the importance of set and setting in maximizing positive outcomes and minimizing potential risks.

Guidelines and Recommendations: Findings from real-world data can contribute to the development of guidelines or recommendations for individuals intending to use psychedelics, emphasizing the significance of preparation, safe environments, and psychological readiness for optimizing experiences.

Challenges and Ethical Considerations

Data Privacy and Ethics:

Ensuring Privacy and Confidentiality: Collecting real-world data necessitates stringent measures to protect the privacy and confidentiality of participants. Ethical considerations are crucial to safeguard the anonymity and well-being of individuals contributing their experiences.

Interpretation and Generalization:

Challenges in Interpretation: Interpreting real-world data requires caution due to the variability in experiences and contexts. Researchers must be mindful of the limitations in generalizing findings and acknowledge the diverse factors that might influence individual experiences.

New treatment modalities

The exploration of psychedelic-assisted therapy as a novel treatment modality for mental health conditions marks a significant shift in therapeutic approaches.

Evolution of Psychedelic-Assisted Therapy:

Treatment Expansion Beyond Traditional Approaches:

Addressing Mental Health Conditions: Psychedelic-assisted therapy represents a departure from conventional treatment modalities. It explores the potential of psychedelics—such as psilocybin, MDMA, and LSD—as adjuncts to psychotherapy in treating mental health disorders like depression, anxiety, addiction, and trauma-related conditions like PTSD.

Revisiting Psychedelics in Therapy: These substances were researched in the mid-20th century for their therapeutic potential but faced legal restrictions and societal stigma, leading to a hiatus in research. Recent scientific interest has revived exploration into their potential therapeutic benefits in controlled settings.

Therapeutic Potential of Psychedelics

Depression, Anxiety, and Addiction:

Psychedelics and Depression: Studies have shown promising results in reducing symptoms of depression. Psychedelics like psilocybin have demonstrated the potential to induce profound psychological experiences that may reset patterns of thinking and provide relief from depressive symptoms.

Anxiety Disorders: Research indicates that psychedelics may alleviate symptoms of anxiety disorders by modulating brain activity and promoting a shift in perspectives, leading to decreased anxiety levels.

Addiction Treatment: Psychedelics, particularly MDMA, have shown potential in assisting addiction treatment by fostering emotional openness and facilitating therapeutic discussions to address underlying issues contributing to addiction.

Exploration in Trauma-Related Disorders

PTSD and Trauma: Recent studies investigating the therapeutic potential of psychedelics, such as MDMA and psilocybin, in PTSD treatment have shown promising preliminary results. These substances might assist in processing traumatic memories and promoting emotional healing within a therapeutic context.

Significance and Future Prospects

Shift in Therapeutic Paradigm:

Holistic and Transformative Approaches: Psychedelic-assisted therapy offers a potentially transformative approach by providing profound psychological experiences that could lead to shifts in perceptions, emotional processing, and behavioral changes, fostering holistic healing.

Research Expansion and Clinical Trials

Growing Scientific Interest: The resurgence of scientific interest in psychedelics has led to increased research funding and clinical trials aimed at understanding their mechanisms of action, safety profiles, and potential therapeutic applications across various mental health conditions.

Challenges and Considerations

Regulatory Hurdles and Public Perception

Navigating Legal Restrictions: Despite promising findings, regulatory frameworks pose challenges in conducting research and implementing these therapies due to the historical classification of psychedelics as controlled substances.

Public Perception and Stigma: Overcoming societal stigma and misinformation surrounding psychedelics remains a challenge, impacting public acceptance and policy considerations.

Improved understanding of the mechanisms of action.

The mechanisms underlying the effects of psychedelics like psilocybin on the brain are complex and not entirely elucidated.

Current Understanding of Mechanisms of Action

Serotonin Receptors Interaction:

5-HT Receptor Activation: Psilocybin primarily interacts with serotonin receptors, particularly the 5-HT2A receptors, leading to alterations in serotonin signaling pathways in the brain.

Neurotransmitter Modulation: Activation of these receptors influences neurotransmitter systems, including serotonin, dopamine, and glutamate, which are implicated in mood regulation, cognition, and perception.

Default Mode Network and Brain Connectivity:

Default Mode Network (DMN): Psychedelics like psilocybin have been observed to modulate the activity of the DMN, a network associated with self-referential thoughts and the resting state of the brain. This modulation may lead to altered perceptions and self-awareness.

Enhanced Connectivity: Some studies suggest that psychedelics may increase neural connectivity between brain regions that don't typically communicate extensively. This enhanced connectivity might contribute to the unique psychological effects experienced during psychedelic states.

Need for Further Research:

Elucidating Complex Mechanisms:

Comprehensive Understanding: Despite advancements, the precise cascade of events triggered by psychedelics in the brain is not fully comprehended. Unraveling the detailed mechanisms involved in their effects, including downstream signaling pathways and neural circuitry alterations, is crucial.

Long-Term Effects and Safety: Understanding the long-term effects of psychedelic use on brain function, neuroplasticity, and potential neurotoxicity remains a significant area requiring exploration. Ensuring the safety and minimizing potential risks associated with their use is imperative.

Impact on Various Mental Health Conditions:

Tailored Therapeutic Approaches: Further research aims to uncover how these substances can be tailored to target specific mental health conditions more effectively. Understanding how psychedelics impact different brain regions in specific disorders could optimize treatment approaches.

Clinical and Practical Applications:

Optimizing Treatment Protocols: Studying the mechanisms of action can aid in optimizing dosages, treatment protocols, and therapeutic regimens to enhance their efficacy while minimizing adverse effects.

Future Research and Challenges:

Advanced Neuroimaging Techniques:

Utilizing Advanced Tools: Advancements in neuroimaging techniques such as functional MRI (fMRI) and PET scans offer opportunities to study brain activity and connectivity changes induced by psychedelics with greater precision.

Ethical Considerations and Regulatory Hurdles:

Ethical Protocols: Ensuring ethical guidelines and participant safety in research studies involving psychedelic substances is crucial. Regulatory obstacles and societal perceptions may pose challenges in conducting comprehensive studies.

Chapter 7

Real-life Transformations and Success Stories

Personal Journeys of Transformation

Psychedelic therapy has shown promise in treating various mental health conditions, including depression, anxiety, and addiction. Here are some personal journeys of transformation, interviews, and success stories showcasing profound changes and healing experiences:

Sarah's story

Sarah, a 35-year-old woman from Chatham, ON, struggled with treatment-resistant depression for years. Traditional therapies and medications provided little relief. However, after learning she can buy magic mushrooms online at Shroom Bros, Sarah experienced a profound shift in her perspective. She began microdosing psilocybin, which helped her change her mind and improve her mental state.

Josh's story

Josh, a 44-year-old business owner, struggled with PTSD and treatment-resistant depression for 44 years. He tried every Rx medication and traditional treatment option before coming down. He attended a legal psilocybin truffle retreat in the Netherlands, which helped him see his heart and soul. He was able to fix it and experience a life-changing transformation.

Case studies

Several studies have shown that psilocybin-assisted therapy can be effective in treating PTSD. An open-label study in traumatized AIDS survivors found that psilocybin-assisted psychotherapy reduced PTSD symptoms, attachment anxiety, and demoralization. Another study found that psilocybin-assisted therapy is effective at treating moderate-to-severe depression in patients with curable and incurable cancer. Depressive symptoms were markedly reduced 1 week and 3 months after high-dose treatment. Marked and sustained improvements in anxiety and anhedonia were also noted.

Real-life transformations

Psilocybin therapy has been shown to induce rapid improvement in depressive symptoms that endure for some weeks. It offers a unique opportunity for introspection and healing. Through relatable characters, vivid descriptions, and compelling plotlines, stories draw individuals into the change journey, making it more relatable and tangible. By appealing to human nature's rational and emotional aspects, stories forge a strong connection, fostering understanding and empathy among stakeholders. They enable individuals to see themselves within the narrative, facilitating a sense of ownership and motivation to embrace the change 167.

Personal journeys of transformation, interviews, and success stories showcase the profound changes and healing experiences that can result from psychedelic therapy. While these stories provide preliminary support for the safety and efficacy of psilocybin and other psychedelics for treating various mental health conditions, further research is needed to better understand the mechanisms of action and the potential risks associated with their use. Psilocybin and other psychedelics are controlled substances in many countries, and their use should only be considered under the guidance of a licensed healthcare professional.

Conclusion

As we conclude this exploration into the transformative power of psychedelic therapy, it becomes evident that the potential benefits of substances like psilocybin extend far beyond conventional treatments for mental health conditions. The journey through this book has illuminated key aspects of their therapeutic capacity and the need for responsible exploration.

Summarizing the Transformative Power:

The narrative woven within these pages sheds light on the profound impact of psychedelic therapy. It emphasizes how substances like psilocybin, when utilized in controlled and therapeutic settings, have shown promise in alleviating the burdens of mental health disorders. From depression and anxiety to trauma-related conditions like PTSD, these substances offer a glimpse into a novel approach to healing, providing insights into their potential to induce profound shifts in perception, emotional processing, and personal growth.

Key Takeaways from the Book's Exploration:

Holistic Healing: Psychedelic therapy offers a holistic approach, addressing not just symptoms but delving into the root causes of mental health disorders.

Mind-Body Connection: Understanding the interconnectedness of the mind and body in the healing process is crucial for optimizing therapeutic outcomes.

Set and Setting: The importance of a supportive environment and mental preparedness, known as set and setting, significantly influences the psychedelic experience.

Encouragement for Further Exploration:

To my readers, this book serves as an invitation to delve deeper into this burgeoning field. However, this journey comes with a responsibility to approach psychedelic exploration with caution and mindfulness. Responsible usage entails:

Education and Preparation: Before considering any psychedelic experience, educating oneself extensively about the substance, its effects, and potential risks is imperative.

Guidance and Support: Seeking guidance from experienced and reputable professionals in controlled settings can ensure safety and maximize the therapeutic benefits.

Integration and Reflection: After the experience, taking time for reflection and integration is crucial. This involves processing and incorporating insights gained into daily life for lasting personal growth.

In closing, while the transformative potential of psychedelic therapy is evident, responsible exploration is paramount. It is a call to approach these substances with reverence, respect, and mindfulness. May this book serve as a catalyst for informed exploration, emphasizing the importance of ethical practices, safety, and respect for the profound nature of the human mind.

As we navigate the uncharted territories of psychedelic therapy, let us walk this path with reverence, embracing the potential for healing and personal transformation while ensuring the well-being of ourselves and our communities.

www.ingramcontent.com/pod-product-compliance
Lightning Source LLC
Chambersburg PA
CBHW060842260726
48661CB00002B/553